Leaving the Hills

For Megan, Ellis, Huw, Tomos and Kate- the future.

Leaving the Hills

Tony Curtis

Seren is the book imprint of
Poetry Wales Press Ltd.
Suite 6, 4 Derwen Road, Bridgend,
Wales, CF31 1LH

www.serenbooks.com
Follow us on social media @SerenBooks

The right of Tony Curtis to be identified as
the author of this work has been asserted in accordance
with the Copyright, Designs and Patents Act, 1988.

© Tony Curtis, 2024.

ISBN: 978-1-78172-742-3
ebook: 978-1-78172-743-0

A CIP record for this title is available from the British Library.

The publisher acknowledges the financial assistance of the Books Council of Wales.

Cover painting: 'Brynteg Lights: The Calennig' by Hanlyn Davies.

Contents

Leaving the Hills

As we are driven away
I watch the Packard's mirrors
Become tiny screens of flames:
The Hollywood Hills ablaze like a film set
With our house, centre focus, being consumed.
Because that is what life does here: consume.

So what is lost?

The last Havanas Groucho gave me
In the box he drew on –
A lady's opera fan, a tenor's waxed moustache
Inked in as if to say, "Whatdya gonna say?"

My mother's Chesterfield, Father's bureau,
Curtains and carpets shipped from Heal's.
A friend's blade from Balliol, the Summer Eights.

Photos:
            Greta in baggy trousers, the face
Of a goddess hidden under the brim
Of a large, floppy hat.

Against the banks of a dried-out river
At one of our picnics two figures – Charlie and Anita –
"The most famous dwarves in the world,"
Cecil called them when he borrowed my Rolleiflex.

Standing before "Personnage et oiseaux"
Russell who, rather dismissively, I recall,
Pronounced that exquisite Joan Miro "playful".
As a great philosopher might.
And all the books:

Isherwood's *Goodbye to Berlin*, inscribed to us,
Wystan's *Poems*, with his constant scratchings-out,
A well-thumbed *Ulysses* from Shakespeare and Co.

The decades of diaries, Maria's and mine,
The manuscripts that would have been my last works,
All overtaken by flames.

And as we were halted at a red light
Before Hollywood Boulevard en route
Rooms hurriedly booked at the Chateau Marmont
I started to float, my body's weight left there
On the cool leather of the limousine.

I felt
Extraordinarily clean, extraordinarily clear.
Given more time,
That could have been a fresh start.

*Aldous Huxley and his wife fled their house in Beachwood Canyon, L.A.
in 1961: it was destroyed by the Bel Air wildfires.*

Longley's Work

Your books I keep
on the shelf beside my pillow;
slim and strong stalks full
of sap and bearing flowers.

It's right to be reminded:
heed to your place,
heed to your people,
be true to your language.

Yours is not my land, Michael,
or places I have been:
Dooaghtry, Inishturk,
Glen Lough, Carrigskeewaun,

Nor would I recognize
your familiars –
golden plover, greenshank, mallard,
the cloud orchid.

Still, I'll open at a random page
this morning, as I do,
splashing the sleep from my face
with the cold, peaty water of your words.

Caroline Gerbola on Conchita

For Peter Lavery

Pod comes running to our gang and says –
'Seamus is catching something amazing
in the yard at the back of O'Leary's!'

And when we got over there we started spying
around the wall to see –
this horse that was white, but not entirely,
with spots and strokes on it as if
a painter had flicked his brush with black and dark greys
over the paper.

A girl on top of him took off her red injun bonnet
and got the horse to bow down to a mat
she'd laid on O'Leary's gravel.
There was no saddle that I could see, but a blanket and furs.

She had cowboy boots and leggings
and held in one hand a silver-topped cane or riding whip.
Her top was nothing to it and sparkly.
'That would be the circus,' said Pod,
but we'd all got that a mile before Pod, who is not the fastest.

'I'm asking my Ma for a ticket,' he says.
But what would we be doing that for
with our money?

We'd seen the best of it –
the beautiful girl, the horse as big as a house
kneeling down for her and for us
because of what her legs had said to it
and her being one and the same with that magnificent beast.

Of Barnacles, Geese and other Wonders

From Gerald of Wales's Travels in Ireland

I send report from this land brought into the true faith
by holy Patrick who, it is said, studied at Saint Illtyd's.
Whereby it is fitting that his countryman be tasked with assessing
the rightfulness of their religion amongst those who share our sea.

This race is inconstant, changeable, wily, and cunning.

There are in this land many birds called barnacles,
which nature produces in a wonderful manner
out of her ordinary course.
They resemble the marsh-geese, but are smaller.

Being at first,
gummy excrescences from branches floating on the waters,
and then enclosed in shells to secure their free growth,
they hang by their beaks, like seaweeds attached to the timber.

Being in progress of time
                        well covered with feathers,
they either fall into the water or take their flight in the free air,
their nourishment and growth being derived,
in this very unaccountable and curious manner,
from the juices of the wood in the sea-water.

I have often seen with my own eyes more than a thousand
minute embryos of birds of this species on the seashore,
hanging from one piece of timber, covered with shells,
and, already formed: these are the very same barnacles.

No eggs are laid by these birds after copulation,
as is the case with birds in general;
the hen never sits on eggs to hatch them;
in no corner of the world are they seen to pair and build nests.

Hence, in some parts, bishops and men of religion
make no scruple of eating these geese on fasting days,
as not being flesh,
                    because they are not born of flesh.

But these men are clearly drawn into error.
For, if anyone had eaten part of the thigh of our first parent,
Adam, which was really flesh although not born of flesh
I should think him not guiltless of having broken his fast.

Repent, all you unhappy infidels,
recollect, though it be late,
our shared Eden:
                    that man was first generated from clay
without being procreated by male and female;
any sensible veneration for the Book
shall not allow you to deny that.

In the second place, woman was generated of the man,
without the intervention of the other sex:
Eve was grafted from Adam by God's hand.

The third mode of generation by male and female alone,
as it is the ordinary one, obstinate as you are,
you unbelievers must admit this to be most natural.

But the fourth, from which alone came our Salvation,
you should learn –
namely, birth from a woman, without union with a man.
I say, you reject Mary
                    to your own perdition.

Blush with shame, you wretches without the faith.
At least admit to the lessons of nature,
which in confirmation of our best teaching,
continually produces and gives birth to new animals
without union of male and female.

             The first creature, Man,
was begotten of clay.
proceeding from the God of nature for once only.
That was a stupendous miracle – rooting us in the Garden;

      this present, though not less admirable, is less to be wondered at,
because imitative nature often performs it:
the shell becomes the goose.

But human kind is so constituted, that it holds nothing
to be precious and remarkable
except what is uncommon and of rare occurrence.
The rising and setting of the sun –
than which there is nothing in the world more beautiful,
nothing more fit to excite our wonder –
we pass by without due admiration,
because they are daily present to our eyes;
while an eclipse of that sun astonishes
because it is so rare in our short lives.

             Mark this:
the procreation of bees from the honeycomb,
by some mysterious inspiration of the sweet breath of life,
appears to be a fact of the same kind
as the origin of these barnacle geese.

Our Lord was born anew
                        after growing on his wood –
the Cross nourished him and nourishes us for eternity –
so then each strangeness, each unexplained creature
is surely coming forth to secure us in our faith.

To walk on the shore and find such as these barnacles
is as much a soul-treasure as our prayers in the cell,
our devotions through the measured day.

We praise our Maker
                        by walking the world.

Climbing the Overhang

at Eglwys Dewi Sant, Carmarthen

Rusted nails, the slip of loosened slates,
Another and another – the place is open to the weather,
Rain from the west, snow from the east
Complete the wrecking work and then it's too late.

The Church throws good money after bad
To patch the holes – a small fortune
Goes up into the clouds that come over the Irish Sea.
So the place is sold. The pews are plastered by pigeons,

The font a dry stone, the pulpit silent and soiled.
The wooden list of the Great War's dead
And the marble plaques to the crachach – Williamses, Pictons,
Davieses – fade back into the dusty shade.

In the churchyard, to the rear and towards the town,
Seven war graves decline, their greying Portland
Headstones sinking into a maze of barbed brambles:
We shall strain to remember them.

Your grandmother and grandfather's marble chips
And small urn persist against the weeds and ivy
Under the ancient yew. You call and tidy up
Each time that you pass through.

Though now you have to negotiate the parked cars,
Families using the climbing and bouldering centre
That rears from the nave and vestry: a church repurposed.
The angled grips and coloured foot-holds pattern the walls

Like stained glass, some star exploding from its last millenium.
The Overhang. It's a tough climb:
Roped and helmeted, harnessed and gloved,
They spider their way to heaven.

The Mayor of Llansteffan

Carmarthen Journal 4 Sept. 1914, p.5:
The following appeal from a Carmarthen boy,
affectionately known as "Bonny",
ought to be irresistible. He writes to us

Comrades, I went up to the Barracks to join the soldiers,
and they refused to do so.
I am a strong listy man, and my age is 24 years,
height 5 foot 9 weight 10st. 7lb.

Why should they refuse me
as Kitchener wants 100,000 men ...
I will do my best to fight for my King and Country
as long as the War will last.

This reported in the phony bluster
at the beginning, long before
Mametz, before they'd welcome
every dull Dai, each stunted Shenkin.

**

Most towns had a character, a Fool, an oddity,
even mine so far from the centre of everything –
wars, rock and roll, the march of history.
We were buttoned up in chapel black and white.

Except for mad Bonny, our freak about town,
loud, clumsy, lolling flaneur
who seven years running was proposed for "mayor"
in the summer carnival down in Llansteffan.

Sixty years on I'm told a story by my cousin:
he died in Lammas Street. Bonny cross-hatched
by his *Evening Post* delivery satchel, drank beer slops
left unfinished by Saturday night farm boys

in the Drovers or the Falcon. They were cruel and wild.
So that Mayor Bonny the man-child
was pushed into the old horse trough and died of cold,
his unsold papers scattered in the wind.

Bonny who was no idiot savant. Bonny
who was shipped home shaking and twitching,
who'd carried shrapnel and gas in his head for years,
which is what we boys laughed at out of fear, and knowing no better.

★★

Another says he was married, had kids,
then it failed, went sour. He was found
in a derelict house down on Quay Street
long gone and chewed by rats as big as trench cats.

"Even' Post, Even' Post" echoes in places few remember,
doorways demolished, lanes paved over, at the old market gate,
and on Nott Square where stands the victor of the Afghan War.
Now his election speeches are forgotten:

Vote for me: Bonny for Llansteffan's Mayor

I promise to build a bridge across the Towy tides
to Ferryside. No cockles will be raked
except they contain pearls; a coracle man will gather
his nets next summer to discover a wife.

My elves will gild the castle turrets each morning.
A heron will swoop down with twins for Mair Ty Mawr
a year after her husband disappeared.
Her Mam will not be struck dumb, but will sing.

Every third Friday fish will fly into the kitchen pan.
The vicar will levitate over the lectern, a foot or more;
Ianto's mare will be delivered of a zebra;
the back road to Llanybri will be paved with gold, you'll see.

Vote for me: Bonny for Mayor.

17

**

So, walking down Lammas Street, pause at the trough:
the sky reflected there is clouded by no dreams,
Bonny's passing stirs no ripple; no horse
or man sups there now. But driving on

to Llansteffan and walking the sands you'll find
his promises are in the wind; now look again –
those are not clouds, but the struts of Bonny's bridge
arching from here to Ferryside and on to the wide world.

Woodham's Scrapyard

Walking through the alleys of rusting locos and tenders
That filled the land between Barry and the Island funfair,
With Gareth over my shoulder and his buggy folded
As we crossed the sidings' sleepers and rails, we lost count
Of the numberless, nameless hulks in that graveyard.
Though some were marked, "for Darlington", "Didcot", "Sold".
One was graffitied "Save me" on the smoke box door.

And among the shunters and nondescript pullers of freight
There'd be a 4-6-0 – a *Hall*, or *Manor* or *Castle* Class,
The sort of distinguished beast that had made my day
Trainspotting on Carmarthen station. That terminus
Had brought my grandfather from farm work in Berkshire
To the point where **G**od's **W**onderful **R**ailway
Split to the north and west, across to the Irish Sea.

Manor Farm, West Ilsley, Newbury
July 19th, 1912.
This is to certify that Jim Curtis has worked for me
For four years. During that time I always found him
A very steady quiet, respectable lad.
                              Edward H. Cory.
So, Jim went west, to Wales and my story began.

We'd see Woodham's hulks towering past our house on lorries,
Creaking their way to enthusiasts in England: heritage teams
Of grinders, fitters, welders, and a bloke who'd sourced that missing,
Crucial bolt. Weekends of welding and painting and dreaming
Of the first head of steam. And, if those men lived long enough, they'd see
A gala opening day, local reporters, regional tv, their families
Realising what all those hours had been about – the first wheels turning.

And is the penny pressed on that first yard of rail
Kept in a grandson's box of treasures?

My inky notebook of numbers is long gone.
A memory of being eleven and old enough to take the train
Up the line to Swansea, on my own. An hour on the station, then back again,

Collecting numbers all the way. And then a Castle pulling in –
Perhaps the one that we walked underneath at Swindon Steam Museum.
Thousands of parts – nut and bolt, boiler and piston –
Each and every one made at that same factory. *Caerphilly Castle*

Shining, impossibly pristine. A museum piece,
One of those not broken for scrap.
And now, where Woodham's acres of iron and rust
For years bled oil and soot and dust into the soil,
It's *The Quays* – rows of starter homes, semis and "executives",
An Asda, a playground with swings, a slide and a goal.
They had to treat the site for years, to clean it up.

In the Fifties, Mr John, next-door to my Gran's,
Dressed as a black-faced minstrel in the carnival every year.
I'd see him walk back from work in the engine-sheds,
Stopping to hawk and clear his lungs into our hedge.
He was as dark as any miner, his face soot-pocked
From crawling through, cleaning the boilers. Riddled with cancer,
He died long before the romance of steam.

At the G6 Face

For Jack Crabtree

Someone has called his name
and you catch him as he turns
away from the coal-face,
his lamped helmet perched back,
eyes squinting in the half light.

Even at the Face, damn near naked,
breathing dust, men are not black.
Their lamps and the Anderton Shearer's glow
shows their skin as a tough, sinewy covering,
a tapestry of flesh tones – brown and red and blue.

The arm muscles flexed and full,
his shoulder is a slag heap with the gorse taking root,
and the rib cage is taut and wiped clean
where the skeleton shows through.

ABERFAN VOICES

After the photographs of I.C. Rapoport, 1966

Ready to Fly

One day, when I'm grown up,
I will fly a real aeroplane
From London or Cardiff or America
And we will fly over Wales
And I will look out the window and point and say,

"Down by there is where we lived,
That little village in a valley.
                                        No
Not that valley, the other one
With the green slopes and the new houses and see –
That new building, the school."

And the sun will shine on the river Taff,
Clean and silver,
With the children playing and fishing.

And being so high, we will have to imagine
The fish they catch.
But we will know the faces of the children.

Delivery

Bent double under that sack
He could be Hercules carrying the bull,

Atlas holding the whole weight
Of the endless heavens, stars grown dark:

But now I see him as St Christopher the Christ-bearer
Crossing the water,

At every step the load growing heavier.
For now he knows that each lump of coal

Is a child, each one in Christ embodied,
And that the crossing will never be done.

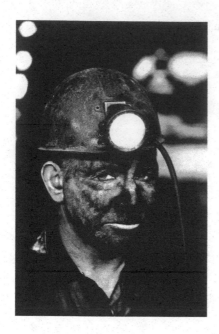

Where I was

Where were you when the old King died?
Walking to the pithead with my butties.

Where were you for the Peace in Our Time?
In the parlour with Delyth and her mother's new wireless.

Where were you when the bombers came?
Holding the hand of a Bevin Boy in the shivering dark.

Where were you when the war ended?
In the bath before our fire, hearing the church bells.

Where were you for the Coronation?
A mile underneath her kingdom.

Where were you when they put a dog in space?
Down here.

What about the missiles in Cuba?
We was well out of reach in the Merthyr Vale: already buried.

Where were you when the President was shot?
Checking my lamp and opening my snap.

And where were you when you heard about Aberfan?
Mid-shift, working at the face, blinded with dust that the tears
Began to wash, and the mandrel dropped
As my fists clenched, and I heard
The distant howls of men.

The Graves

Last night's snow turning to mush,
Except at the height of the tips
Where nothing as pure and white
Should ever rest again.

This grave was a hard cold slog,
But I am used to the work
And three score years and ten has a rightness.
There's been too much digging

For the children's graves where freesias,
Chrysanthemums and lilies were left.
And now in the rain and snow
They curl and brown and wither.

We had extra help in for that. Other firms.
But I still have the memory of their weight in my arms.

He Being Dead Yet Speaketh

Most of the time his eyes were closed,
His hands were clasped to the pulpit,
Or he held on to the Bible
Like a buoy to keep him afloat.

Was there ever a sermon dug so deep
From the heart of a preacher?
He gave his son....
Loudly, through our tears we sang for all of them.

The First Baby

On a bed made up before the fire
In our front room
Our new baby is washed and fed
And put to sleep alongside Mam
In the light of the window.

A bit of sun comes through our nets
And makes funny shadows
And patterns on Mam and baby.

Mam says his eyes are not really open
And he can't know his brother yet.
Only light and shadows and shapes.
Not the dark houses I can see down our street
Like a ghost street, spooky through the nets.

The Mackintosh Hotel

The Mac is where we go to get away.
It's always been at the centre of everything:
The Chapel and the Mac –
One for giving and one for taking away.

The crooner over from Caerphilly
Was pre-booked, but kept it low and sentimental like.
Bottles of stout, Hancock's bitter, a game
Of darts, the kids fumbling and cuddling.

Keeping it normal, because carrying on is best.

'Til Geraint tipped one too many down his neck,
Drowning the singer with Men of Harlech
And then gets up to do the Twist.
On his own, eyes closed,

With the whole place watching him.
And then he does a striptease
And that's when we knew something had really changed.
And would never be the same.

Dannie's Rock

i.m. Dannie Abse

Countless low tides leaving the Ogmore beach wide
For walks, French cricket and burying fathers.

Out to the west, half way to England, it seems,
The sea baring its black teeth shows Tusker Rock,

Ynys Twsgwr, *tu skar*, stark above the flat water,
Fangs shown only because of the wrecks –

A wheelhouse, ribs, blown open boiler room,
Propellor, capstan, winch and chains,

The long-broken spine of the S.S. Liban lost in a storm,
And many others. The dead sailors and a child,

All those who floundered, drowned, falling
From the tilting decks to their cold deaths.

A colony of starfish and mussels and goose barnacles
Live and prosper on what we leave.

The sea scans the same measured syllables,
Songs that sound out of the scored waves.

There are more stories to tell – Britten, Debussy,
Always more music to raise from the chains of the deep;

For these blind rocks, Dannie,
Could never satisfy the hungers of our sea.

The Guardian

Every other morning, I take the longer walk
for the paper –

over the stone bridge and up Constitution Hill,
round the path at the back of the top houses

and between the trees
down to the river again,

the walkers' wooden bridge, the children's playground,
and then on to the high street.

Even on cold and wet days,
I have to check our bridge over the Thaw.

Sparrows bicker in the bankside bramble,
cream and pink cattle grazing the slopes below the castle,

last week a moorhen skittered, and today, downstream,
an unseen heron, startled, flaps up and away

out of the trees' shadows and on
towards the church, or the roofs in Llanblethian.

Upstream, a dabbling Mallard tails up out of the water,
but, still, there's no flicker of the rumoured trout.

A year now of looking: no glint or glide,
no ripples rising to the evening flies.

I shall persist: the priestly heron
is surely proof of fish. I'll take it for a sign.

Bosherston Pike

Our Lady of the muddy depths, angling through the lily roots,
Razor teeth and steel-clasp jaws
Cruising the pools like a U-Boat in the shadows.

Each season she folds her orange eggs into the tangle of stalks
But in a harsh winter will, with that twisting muscled neck,
Eat her own, and anything that moves.

Three men work through this autumn afternoon –
Spinners, jerkbait, glinting spoons
Creasing through the Indian Summer warmth.

She keeps you waiting, wears you down with the little perch
And roach that she turns her snout from, avoiding the fight,
Small offerings she gives up from her pool.

But then you'll strike and pull into the light
This memory of ancient beasts and weapons, spiked, scaled,
Ridged with menace, though a fine olive and silver in the sun.

And as you land her, you take the full heft now
Of that packed flesh and muscle, before slipping her back in,
Her mucus on your hands, something older than we know.

Flying the Lanner

A ball of clawed and beaked fluff in the cage:

first she must walk
and then run
and then learn to fly
but only to Griff, who is her mother
and the only mother she will ever know.

There is no love lost
for Griff's voice and whistle mean food –
day-old chicks, yellow and fresh and soft –
a gloved banquet until she is fed up
and needs to do no more.

Griff's love is real, an arm's length love,
an arm-long perch she'll fly to,
land on, ride on claw-tight.
All this is to come; first she'll cast her fluff and grow,
stiffen her bones and press out her wings:

the most exquisite patterning, the most precise
engineering. She'll scuttle
across the grass after him, blink
at the endless sky, follow that chick smell,
until she's ready for him to fly her.

Then the cast of the lure, the widening gyre
the soft flesh and early bones,
as her reward. She'll bounce her weight
on his arm, grip the glove,
safe in her hoodwinked love.

Belgian Hares

On the drive from Pilkem to Artillery Wood
In the wide field's stubble we see a hare
Rise up from its haunches,
Stand tall, then with sinewy legs

Stretching and pumping, bound
Directly into a solid wall of ripe corn
To disappear.
There is no metaphor here.

That July at Charleston

Serving dinner Grace looked upset: it seems
the village has had two telegrams today.
Duncan says with the harvest and the hay,
they are already lacking the men.

Virginia helped Grace clear things away,
which is certainly unusual.
Some thirty miles across the Channel
England is piling up its dead.

Had we not heard the big guns
carried on an East wind?
At breakfast the tea spoons had rattled again
on our saucers, Vanessa said.

Claude and Chouchou at Le Moulleau, 1916

It is cool beneath the pines where they sit
after their hard climb over the Dune du Pilat
with their picnic under its cloth in the basket.
A father and daughter in the sea breeze
and shadows — En blanc et noir.

He still wears a striped, light summer suit,
bow tie and a straw boater, but his eyes
are furrowed behind his wire-framed glasses.
Chouchou in a white, loose dress and her large, floppy hat
with the white flower appliquéd; her holiday shoes
from which she has shaken the sand.

The sound of the sea-shore soothes —
they are two years into a war that may never end;
he has cancer and she will die of diphtheria within a year.
But for this afternoon the sun swims through the trees;
she will close her eyes and hear the Atlantic playing its etudes
and her father's La Mer.

They are miles further south from la cathédrale engloutie,
the rough coast and myths of Brittany.
High above this town is Notre-Dame des Passes;
they have climbed all those church steps and looked across
at Cap Ferret's lighthouse, its red dome bright
against the two clear blues of sky and sea.

Everything will be precious from this day,
these hours taken from painful times.
As Emma's camera fixes their lives in this moment
their dog has heard something in the pines
and turns its head to look away.

Madame des Lapins

Our first few summers over here it was groundwork,
Fixing the roof and pointing the old stones.
The house had been abandoned from way back,
So we could afford it, but were there for the long haul.

Everyone smiled or shrugged, no problems
With the locals even before we became locals.
Monsieur Boussac in the old farm down the track
Was patient with our school French and the endless paperwork;

Who in the local market was recommandé and which stalls were rusé.
Though we found everything was so cheap, and authentic.
His three remaining cows gave us milk, there was cheese from his cousin.
Sue started to turn the ground behind our sagging barn into a garden.

"Madame Lablais – Vous devez lui rendre visite."
He gestured beyond the wood. "C'est une sorciére," then
Kissed his fingers like a gourmet in a bad film:
"Légumes, prunes, poires, lapins.

"Lapins." It was years since we'd had rabbit at home.
Who caught rabbits? Though after the war Sue's father
Had a ferret and a terrier and put meat on the table from
His nets staked over the warren between them and the railway line.

We walked up through the woods and Madame met us at her gate.
She pointed to her barn and when she swung open the doors
The place was full of rabbits fenced in, a hundred or more –
Bugs Bunny, Thumper, Roger Rabbit.

They had straw and the tops of greens and cabbages were strung
From the rafters. They jumped and seemed happy
To nibble at the food. No need for dogs or ferrets, here,
They were kept and fed and knew no better.

Madame stepped over the wire and they came to sniff at her boots.
She bent down to stroke them, then picked one,
Lifted it into her arms and cwtched it like a kid or a lamb.
"C'est Espoire, ma petite," she said and led us out into the yard.

There were barrels, a stack of old tools and a Labourier tractor
Which hadn't moved for years. It must have puttered past Panzers
Hidden under the cover of the woods for the counter-attack.
It lacked one tyre and its seat had fallen to the ground.

"Il est trés historic," I said, feeling stupid. "Oui. Dans les années quarante,"
And without breaking stride Madame swung the chosen one
By its legs against the engine cowl and brained it.
On her kitchen table she skinned and wrapped it in newspaper.

"Soixantes francs, s'il vous plait, Monsieur, Madame."

"Ca va?" said Monsieur Boussac on our return.
We showed him the rabbit's tidied joints and he gave a nod.
The neat rib-cage and the separated flattened little liver –
"Très special pour vous. Bon appétit," she'd said.

We offered him the parcel, but he waved us away,
"Moutarde, vin rouge – un très bon repas."
So I cooked it in our Le Creuset, but Sue couldn't touch it.
I said, "Look, it's less cruel than suckling pig or foie gras."
We eat what we have to eat – Stalingrad, the Irish Famine.
At the end, in St Malo when the Germans locked the gates and battened down
Against that terrible bombing, there was no cat, dog or rat to be seen.
Just "Lapins du Boche," the bones picked clean.

Kate's Hare

When they visit she likes to pick up pots and shells
and re-arrange the framed family photographs.
Can I hold the rabbit, Tadcu?
Of course, she can, but, Look at those ears – it's a hare.
Solid chrome by Louis Lejeune, standing tall
with its thread for screw-fixing to the radiator cap
of the pre-war Alvis we had sometime in the Fifties
sequence of Ford Prefects, Austin Sevens, Morris Minors.

Tadcu, tell me why the hare's car had a hole in the floor.
And again, I try to explain about the footwell in the back,
how that would have been for her brogues
after walking the estate, shooting, or at the hunt; high heels
slipped off on the way back from the mayor's ball.
But I could park my Dinky cars down there and drive them with my toes.
I'd stand on the seat exchanging salutes with the AA man on his motorbike;
but cwtch down on worn leather for Radio Luxembourg's Top Twenty in
the dark.

All our expeditions were logged by my mother in a book–
from Carmarthen the long way around the Severn,
through Gloucester and up the Air Balloon to the cousins in Newbury.
West to the cousins in Kilgetty and Pwllcrochan
through Bancyfelin and Llanddowror's dark wood,
then Llanteg and the county line where, my father declared,
the weather always became Pembrokeshire fine.
Once to Lynton and Lynmouth to see the devastation of the flood.

All this, like the hare, has too much weight
when I hand it to her,
its long ears crossing at the tips, alert,
its haunches and its front paws ready to spring.
She needs both hands to hold the Alvis mascot,
which must feel dead, like a cold silver thing
from a distant life, and will not easily travel
across the years to where we are.

The Trials of Anne James

Culm and coal we dig out
But I never saw the like of that raised
From the Roarer Pit
Close by Hook on that afternoon in July.

Anne James was spied near the old coal bank
Staring at the sky.
And there being a baby's cry heard by a passing oxen boy
He told the tale and thems from Freystrop come out
To discover.
                    But 'twas the wrong workings
At Nash Wood and they did find the child closer to Hook
When a collier, David Golland, winched down some seventy feet
Was brought back up holding a check apron and kerchief
Wrapped about a girl.
The child was taken to Mary Halfhead who kept it for the coroner.

~~~

James Barrah: I have known the prisoner for seven years; she was in my
service for nearly two years. I remember on the 27th July last, while work-
ing with me, she complained of a headache. She then worked at a pit about
a mile from her home.   She asked leave to go home, and I gave her leave.
She left about twenty minutes before four, and went towards her own
home. I know Nash Wood, but not the Dungeon-hill field. Nash Wood
lies right in her road home. I observed her to be with child.

~~~

And Mary Pritchett spoke of finding blood ten yards from that pit,
So it may be believed that Anne, unprepared,
Though big with child,
Did drop the same.
                    And that it rolled in to the pit.

~~~

Hester Thomas cross examined:
I knew she was in the family way,
Although she never spoke to me about it.
On the night she came to my house,

I saw taken out of her pocket
Two little caps
A belly band
A forehead piece
And a shirt.
Which were things for a new-born child.
She told me her child was dead-born.

~~~

The next day, I, my brother, and Mr. Phillips examined the body,
And we were of an opinion that respiration had taken place.
It is possible a woman may be delivered at standing,
The navel string would inevitably be broken.
And the child may fall to the ground and occasion a fracture of the skull,
Sufficient to cause death,
                              but I won't say immediate death.

~~~

Geo. L. Millard, Esq: I was present at the coroner's inquest in Haverford-
west, and saw the child; I examined it, and found two bones of the skull
broken, and a great extravasation of blood in the brain. Both bones in a
direct line from the crown of the head towards the ear were broken. The
umbilical cord was not severed. The child was full grown. It was a female
child. In my judgment it was born alive. In my judgment the extravasation
of blood on the brain was the cause of its death.

~~~

Anne James working the winch,
Nine months gone and unmarried:
The sun cooking, her womb an oven.
The handle brushing her belly
At every turn.
                    At every turn
Her arms and back complain.
Each bucket of coal a blackness that blinks
As it's born into the light of its first day.

Jury: Acquitted of willful murder, but guilty of child concealment: one year.

41

Events at Carmarthen: 18th September, 1829

On Monday last the extreme penalty of the law was carried into effect
on David Evans, for the wilful murder of Hannah Davies, seventeen,
on the drop in the County Gaol, in the presence of the assembled town.

Since the evening of his conviction, this unfortunate man
had been penetrated with a just sense of the enormous weight
of the crime he committed, and of the need for unaffected penitence

as a means of regaining that divine favour betimes
which he had forfeited and which shall surely be returned
to those who acknowledge the true darkness of their crimes.

As soon as he saw that his doom was inevitably fixed, they say
his firmness forsook him, and he sought in prayer and devotional exercises,
that hope and that consolation which this world cannot give nor take away.

The victim unsuspected and confiding, fell by that arm
which ought to have cherished and protected her from harm.
Her lover was her murderer, he first seduced, and then hurried her

"with all her imperfections on her head," into the presence of her Creator,
without a moment to offer an ejaculatory prayer for mercy,
for when she fell under the assassin's blows, no cries did she utter.

This unhappy man, who has now expiated with his life
the violation of the law of nature and religion, has made a full
disclosure of the facts connected with this horrible tragedy,

and has acknowledged the justice of his sentence. In gaol
he was attended by ministers of various denominations,
to impart those required spiritual consolations:

'And if external contrition, and a diligent appliance to prayer be
taken to indicate internal change, there is every reason to hope
that he is a new creature, and that he will not perish everlastingly.'

At the appointed hour, at the drop at Carmarthen Gaol,
when the Reverend Jones did let fall his 'kerchief,
the wretch fell, only for the scaffold to snap and fail.

In shock, the harrowed feelings of the assembled throng
was evidenced in a groan, not loud but deep. He fell
to the platform, but did not receive any bodily wrong.

The scene at this moment was painfully distressing.
Evans was impressed with a belief that his life would be spared
in consequence of the abortive first hanging,

and when urged to reascend the drop,
he exclaimed in broken English, "No hang again – no, no,
no gentlemen was no hang twice for same thing, stop!"

He resisted the re-execution of the sentence, until he could see
that force would be resorted to, so again ascended the drop,
and was launched without a struggle into eternity.

After remaining suspended an hour, he was cut down,
and after being dissected was placed in a coffin
left open to public inspection, and thousands availed themselves

to view the mortal remains of this ill-fated young man.
Thus, there were three deaths at this time,
for Hannah was found by the doctor to be four months gone,

for which reason Evans had least cause to destroy her,
but for which very reason, it is clear,
he shamefully did commit that crime.

Glyn Jones at Llansteffan

On this cloudless day in early May
when the river Towy is silvered in the sun
you and Doreen are ashes and dust
resting under the small slate with your names
outside the door of the stoned martyr St Stephen's;
a short ride from Llanybri,
the village of your birth in 1903
and a stretch further from Fern Hill's farm.

Snug under your stone, Glyn,
snug beneath the castle
the sheltered side of its hill
that you and Dylan climbed to reach Laugharne.
You rang the ferryman's bell to row you across the Taf
to where your young friend would later lodge
in his heron heaven, his un-priested hell.

Glyn, you would have loved the gifts of this morning –
the bowed over daffodils, wild garlic's sweet stink,
the sun setting on fire the east window by John Petts,
orange and red making the altar stained glass;
the Towy on the turn becoming sea –
west to the island of Caldey
where David Jones found some peace
after the trenches and Mametz;
and east to Worms Head, Rhossilli –
where Dylan and his Little Cough, George Hooping,
rode to the dashing sea on the roof of a lorry.

When I asked you at the end,
pillow-propped in your final bed,
if you still believed in God,
you smiled: "Often," you said.
I know that you would wish your two-tongued dragon,
y ddraig gyda dwy iaith,
to stir itself this fine morning, Glyn,
then rage among these gentled dead.

The Rising of the Rivers

Today the Taf's lost
itself in the marsh pastures
between St Clears and Llanddowror.

It was always thus in those long winters
of my boyhood journeying down to the cousins
in the bay of cockles,

but now we see clearly,
from the high arc of this new road,
it has spilled from its meanderings

to lake over the fields
up to the edges of this raised passage:
this would have drowned the old road.

How long before the overspill
reaches Laugharne and the sea,
islanding the hamlets and farms?

The Gronw, Wenalt, Fenni and Cywyn
rising in the Preselis and the Fans,
the crooked streams becoming the Taf and Cynin,

all sluicing down to the Boathouse and Castle,
challenging the tide coming over
the heron and wader sandflats of the bay.

Returning the Stones

In later years, retired and free, they'd come down
for quiet weekends, mid-week breaks, out of season
the small hotel between the church and castle,
or B&Bs in the villages along the coast,
so this place could be claimed as their own.

Walks on this beach determined by the time it took
to find a stone or pebble that was heart-shaped
or approximated to the heart: love's old game.

                    At home
they'd placed each one on the mantelpiece, and dressers
until the collection had spilled out into the flower-border,
heart pebbles arranged as a larger heart shape,
prompts to recall their visits,

to remember the seasons –
the sea and sky that stretched all the way to America,
flat and calm for thoughts, or crashing over the headland
so that the waves' rough edge left brown foam at their feet;
the dog walkers giving up,
a young couple turning away from the weather,
running back to the car, hand in hand.

And once on a cold morning in March
the young woman who'd ridden down on her chestnut
appearing behind them so quietly,
soft hooves on the sand to plash,

plash, plash, plash through the shallows
until the sea swelled up to its fetlocks.
Taking time to stare out towards the unreachable island
before cantering the length of the beach back to the farm lane.

She'd said to him:
Flowers and fruit
you can cut and take:
stones are only borrowed.
Her ashes are miles inland, under the ground
at the childhood church to which she'd returned of late.

He has resolved now on each visit to bring them back:
all of them, the heart-shaped pebbles they'd taken,
breaking up the pattern, a handful at a time.

On flat days like this, he stands at the edge
and skims them – three, six, ten kisses with the sea
before going down to the place it has chosen for them.

Look on small, beautiful things

From Rozanne Hawksley (1931-2022)

The herringbone stitch is a holding stitch:
what better to hold than a bone?
I am well practised.

Tiny bones from found, fallen birds and animals
assembled to draw attention to their delicate,
amazing constructions and design.

Often so seemingly fragile, they are strong
for their purpose as well as finely shaped,
They are our scale and form. Bones hold us.

A bird's skull, the spine of a fish, the teeth of a young fox,
pale against each cream calico canvas
to which they are held by my threads.

I believe they are reflective pieces,
little calm icons for the inhabitants of what we call
our world, the Earth.

Picked clean, I choose them for their shape
which is the fact of them, what is left of life.
That may instruct us.

    I do

            not

        name them

    See
            they shape
                    the music
of themselves.

In the Conwy Valley

A bronze fox runs across the headlights
through the pines
under a waxing gibbous moon
netted in the branches.

This crisp and clear November night
welcomes such blessings.
And in the morning our drive home
has a palette of browns, yellows, greens and greys.

On the road to Llangollen, looking back
Eryri is golden under the almost clear sky,
from Yr Wyddfa to Carnedd Llewelyn
the peaks and slopes attend to the day.

There our painter friends and my family quarried:
sheep and slate and light will not be hurried.

The Nant Ffrancon Valley

Peter Prendergast

the challenge of the awe you feel
    the blank sheet
        stroked and pressed
with colours
        edged in black
softened with mist
  turned by the wind's gusts

the harsh gleaming outcrops
    ice carved
  holding the clouds' weight
      that forced down the streams
to make the Ffrancon river
         and settled the Ogwen lake

the memory of the sharp edges
    the stubborn slate
  the yielding
        moss and heather
under your feet that fed
  through the whole of you
to guide the pencil and charcoal
    impression

marks of our being here
  the journey

then you paint a psalm
the stained-glass angling and fracturing
    of the light
and its colours to re-form the world
      in a God-given matter-of-fact vision
            of the gashed glory

    leaving the hills
the painting takes its life out of
    and beyond the valley
to root in the soul of anyone who would
      care to look
again

if you could pull the earth back
you would find out where the world came from

Crack and Warp Column

after David Nash

He cut through bark and trunk
   to open the wood's rings,
       its map of years
to the air and light
       they've grown from,
what the tree closed in on itself
       for a lifetime in that Wenvoe copse.

The angling of his saw called
      wind and dust
         into the core, the journey of his touch,
   the shapes
      the wood instructed him to see:
   a whirling prayer wheel of natural energy

Man-sized,
       this column has given up its sap,
   has hardened and wrinkled
      to that essence.

Now as each day's light moves
        across the glass,
as each night cools the building, the wood
   shifts.
As each person passes,
    breath and flakes of skin
   float and catch in the rough surfaces.

Our witness, our sentry –
        show us what he found in you.

Nature to Nature

Black pyramid, black globe, black cube:
these three charred elm pieces
standing before three charcoal drawings
are for each elemental shape.
We must not touch in this exhibition,
none except for the blind woman
whose hand is guided to the surface of the cube
and palms its splits and whorls.

I wish her taken to his wood, Cae'n-y-Coed,
wrapped against the Winter, standing
for the first half-hour of a snow-fall
in his planted square of tall, straight birch,
feeling the snow lodged in the curls of bark,
and through the shock of cold
seeing one white against another white
through the chilled knowing of her touch.

David Nash retrospective in the National Museum of Wales

POEMS FOR THE PAINTER HANLYN DAVIES IN NEW ENGLAND

At Brynteg Road: Measuring the Years

In the Front Room the calennig hangs
And swings in the angled light,
Your father's token for the New Year.
Only you know the meaning of that.

The Staffordshire Dog on your mantle-piece
Sees everything. Chipped and worn, it is impassive,
A witness as you open your Valentine
To find a dead rat.

The trees they brought in each Christmas
Have become a stark, two-dimensional stencil.
Trace its outline, press through to the uncertain past
With a sharpened pencil. Follow the shape of things.

Through the tunnels of memory
Ride your camels, sail your ships out to sea.

alphaomegalullabylament

That noise is not the wind tonight.
It is the scuffle and squawk of the crows
As they descend the chimney to burst
Out of the fireplace and into your Best Front Room.

They bring their unforgiving beaks,
The soiled feather dusters of their wings,
The sooty shit they'll drop across the swirls
And patterns of your mother's well-kept carpet.

From the ordered, angular tiles of the hearth's
Mouth comes a black, relentless scream.
You shush them away, light an unseasonal fire:
Their lice remain for weeks.

Hand Mirror

And may not a hand mirror
Give back more than an image?

May it not be the source of more light,
Of more than light?

A beacon, an aerial, a web of insights?
At the edges darkness lightens to grey.

Its beveled border and tooled silver back
Turned every day into a kaleidoscope of angles.

When she held it the room splintered
Then became the centre of everything.

A Rebours/Spectre Flush

Against the rain-dropped glass
Is pressed a face, or the form of a face,
Plump, distorted, bound by lattice-work,
That a child might draw to appease its nightmares.

This is a man looking at himself,
Looking at what he will certainly become:
Bereft of hair, ears indistinct; his nose a framed
Garden of delights, colours rioting against the grey.

His mouth is a winter pool caught
Shimmering by the last crystals of frost;
His eyes so tightly closed
He can see beyond any gaze he held.

No, this is the man you may never have been
Pressed against the glass of the actual.
He will not be let in. He must hold
To the plane of the rained-on window.

There are memories, and the possibility
Of memories. Which of us in a dark glass
Has not seen time's servant staring,
Eyes closed into his death mask?

Leather Chair with a Portrait of Marion

after Charles Burton

Then I was shown into this room
Filled with morning light
So that as I stood I took it all in:

The hedge and the trees framed by an Edwardian bay,
A line of jugs and bottles arranged on the sill
– ceramics and glass – which left gaps for meaning.

A worn rug on the blue-painted floor boards,
But principally the chair and a propped painting.
The woman in the painting looking

At me standing before the closed door.
The chair is Bauhaus steel tubing and leather,
Classic but well worn.

An empty chair is an interrogation.
Shall I sit?
Is that required?

With my back to the window and the world,
The sun would warm the nape of my neck.
The leather would begin to learn my shape and weight.

My arms resting on the arms:
I would be facing this door.
I would see what was about to happen.

A JAZZ SUITE

Billie Holiday

Good Morning Heartache, Don't Explain.

Her voice was honey and sour lemons,
smoke-filled clubs and barbed wire.

That first gardenia pinned in her hair
drew blood as it pierced her head

and all the beauty in her life
was cut through with pain.

The men had come and the men had gone
for love is a faucet that turns off and on.

Lover Man, You Let Me Down, Mean to Me.

An unlicensed singer, a junkie handcuffed to the hospital bed,
a roll of fifty dollar bills strapped to her thigh.

Her voice had run itself down to a bad memory –
Prez was not there to rescue his Lady Day.

The pushers, the whorehouse tricks she'd been tutored in
used her up, leaving her crying on empty,

dying in the summertime of fifty-nine
in the Metropolitan Hospital, Manhattan.

Strange Fruit, Fine and Mellow, No Regrets.

The Last of Scott LaFaro

What survived your death on the road from Geneva
Was the Prescott double bass from 1825
Made by that master luthier in Concord, New Hampshire.

Ebony and maple inlay, strengthened neck of slab-cut fir,
Pulled scorched from the wreck you died in, going
Off the highway into trees that night towards Flint

On Route 20 that stretches from East coast to West.
The charred remains identified by your St Christopher;
Your last gig – Newport Jazz with Stan Getz blowing.

But what lives is the trio's final set at the Vanguard
In the Village two weeks before: inspired Bill Evans,
His hands, your hands in dialogue, with Paul Motian
Teasing and brushing the hi-hat and skins,

You underpinning the melody, counter to the tune.
Oh to have been that downtown girl at the corner table
Swirling her Manhattan over ice, caught up in your playing,

Feeling your bass rhythms enter her soul,
Cold shouldering the clutz who was paying,
And sensing the promise of better things. 1961, June,

With Kennedy still reaching for the New Frontier,
Rushing towards our cool future's glow:
Milestones. Detour Ahead, My Man's Gone Now.

Chasin' the Bird

Bird riding the subway 'round midnight, into the early hours,
Times Square…23rd…Christopher Street…34th and Penn,
Washington Square…Columbus, on bourbon and heroin,
Switching cars and lines without purpose or sense,
The subway rails playing be-bop as he went.

And washing up in a club where Dizzy
Was at the bar checking out a new band.
'Help me, Dizzy, why don't you save me?
These kids can play, but now people just come to me
To see the world's most famous junkie.'

Then a cab to the Rothschild Baroness at the Stanhope Hotel.
She called for a doctor, but Bird refused to go,
Just kept watching tv, the Dorsey Brothers Show,
That big band cruising and a guy who could juggle.
On her silk chaise longue Charlie's heart gave up the struggle.

Still grieving his baby daughter, gone the year before,
His life had fallen apart.
The hole in her heart was a horn he wanted to blow life into,
Until his own heart played out. The autopsy report
Described a man of sixty. Charlie "Bird" Parker was thirty four.

Scattering Stan Getz

East of the sun and west of the moon
Go your ashes into the endless Pacific
Off the coast of Malibu in blazing, blue June.
Friends and family on a yacht
That rides the swell of the ocean's swaying
Bass line. With your record playing –

Billy Strayhorn's *Blood Count*
Blocking out the gulls and the waves:
Over the melancholy matter of goodbyes, life blown defiant.

'I've got a big sound. It's deceptively mellow but it carries.'
It's night music, the sad music of the going man.
Then ashes poured from your saxophone case by your grandson.

Brubeck at St David's Hall, Cardiff

An old man walks slowly across the stage,
So stiff and tired that it seems
He will not make it to the Steinway.
The hall is so quiet: it takes an age.

He sits and as he touches the keys
The audience rises to its feet, comes alive:
Five-four, five-four, five-four, five-four, five-four
– *Take Five*.

The Song Prize

If you could choose the time and the place,
The occasion, the final bow,
Would it be here in the concert hall
Sitting in the fourth row,
Just as the Chinese tenor had begun
Serenade Toscane?

O you whom an enchanting dream rocks,
you sleep quietly alone in your bed,
wake up, look at the singer,
slave to your eyes, in the clear night!

And that Faure the last thing you'd heard
As your failing heart's loud snoring
Brings the whole thing to a stop;
The pianist and tenor, both shaken, ushered from the stage,

The wind fractures my voice and the night is frosty

Two doctors from the audience
Lay you down in the aisle,
Then the paramedics, still in their cycle helmets,
Take turns to press down some last chance
Of life into your chest.

It had all been too much of a rush,
A string of business calls,
The log-jammed traffic and then the two of you
Scrambling into your seats with apologies,
Just before the tenor and pianist entered to applause.

But then the performance stopped by the noise you made,
Your collapse and their laying you down;
With you dead or dying as the seats emptied
And the audience were ushered to the bar.

An hour later and you were gone:

Mon chant s'éteint en un accent suprême,
Ma lèvre tremble en murmurant, je t'aime,
Je ne peux plus chanter!

Was that in your head as you drifted away
To where there is no more song?

After worried drinks, the audience was summoned back:
Applause, loud and long,
We sensed that this was the winner.
And when he'd finished, he cried.

Yosemite

Clouds Cristo-wrap El Capitan
and erase the top of the Falls;
then an afternoon of heavy rain.
After the *Monologue from the Oregon Trail*

we go out of the theatre into a pitch night
that the rain has washed clear,
stare up through the huge pines and meet
a sky that comes down to greet us

with its diamonds closer,
bright and sharp and beyond number,
met as if for the first time. As if,
crossing prairies and mountains seeking a new life,

this was the sign to put down roots: here,
and they saw exactly where they were.

Railroad

Between Philadelphia and Penn
Station, New York City,
the black conductor and I
bond, for half an hour maybe,
longer than both fights took,
over memories of Cassius Clay
shaking Liston and the watching world.

First, the wrenched shoulder in Miami
with Liston quitting on his stool.
And then the K.O. in Maine,
except no-one saw that punch;
it eluded cameras and reporters.
'The Mob fixed it. Crazy odds – seven to one.
Sonny died in Vegas, a needle in his arm.'

Who knows the whole story? Who cares now?
The gruesome Sonny Liston,
America's worst nightmare, felled like a bull.
Clay was booed all the way to the ring,
his slave name ringing out still,
but left it as a champion called Ali,
bringing us together decades on.

This train goes underground,
beneath the Hudson River,
under the skyscrapers,
unseen into the heart of the city:
Madison Square Garden –
blood and dreams. Everything we need
it seems.

NAMING JIMMY WILDE

The Tylorstown Terror.

In the ring at the National Sporting Club in 1919
He shook the hand of the Prince of Wales,
Edward the Eighth to be,
'Good work, Jimmy, very well done,'
Having beaten Joe Lynch, a tough Irish-American,
After fifteen bloody rounds.
The hall heavy with cigar smoke,
The tiers of bow-tied gentlemen,
Polite applause, the ranks of toffs, Masons,
And cheering from the crowds outside in Covent Garden,
All for Jimmy.

Three years before, at Holborn Hall,
Young Kid Zulu, a New York Italian,
Went down in the Eleventh
And Jimmy became the Flyweight king of the world.

He took the morning train back to Wales
With the Belt wrapped in his suitcase,
Bought a farm, enlisted and served in uniform as a PT instructor,
One of the Famous Six, putting on shows for the Tommies.

Edward, Prince of Wales, the Welch leek in his cap,
Was still in uniform when he shook Jimmy's hand;
Twenty years later he would shake the hand of Adolf Hitler.

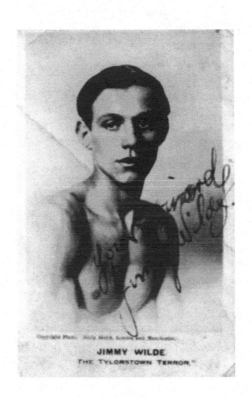

JIMMY WILDE.

"THE TYLORSTOWN TERROR."

The Mighty Atom.

In America they had no chance:
I knocked them all cold in America.

For months in 1919 from city to city,
Coast to coast, they were lining them up
And Jimmy, the champion, was knocking them down.

Then over again in '23, with Lisbeth that final time,
One more big pay day, his title at stake.
First Class: New York, on the Cunard Aquatania.
She'd carried the wounded back from the Dardanelles.

The young Filipino Pancho Villa beat him up,
Cut him down, a right hook he never saw,
At the Polo Fields on the Upper East Side
Where, three years before,
Ray Chapman of the Cleveland Indians
Was killed by a ball from the Yankees' pitcher Carl Mays.

The double-tiered stands and the bleachers were packed,
Up on Coogan's Bluff lights winked from the Mansions.
Jimmy's face hit the canvas and he stayed down in the Seventh.

In that ring, three months later,
Jack Dempsey, the Manassa Mauler,
Beat Luis Ángel Firpo, El Toro Salvaje de las Pampas,
A fight George Bellows would witness and then paint:
With Dempsey knocked out of the ring at the end of the First
To land next to the sketching artist.
Helped back in, he felled the bull in the Second.

Pancho was really Francesco Guillado, out on the Town
For two days after the fight, leeches, cronies and hoods
His companions, Miss New York on his arm.
Hot summer nights in the Bronx
With a stench coming from the streets
And not a breeze off the East River.
But nobody painted that.

The Ghost with a Hammer in his Hand.

Today under the low winter sunshine
Jimmy lies with Lisbeth in the Barry Cemetery

A little old man beaten senseless by yobs
At Cardiff Station waiting for the last train.
He never came back from that low blow.

Fifty years before he would have seen them off,
Knocked them out cold one by one,
Stopping for a cuppa and starting up again
Under the fairground lights, bare-knuckled,
Making more in a night than a week in the pit.

You have to search for his plot, just grass
With a simple, faded marble headstone.
In this section the roots of the pines tilt the graves;
The shadows are long, the ground is uneven
And seems to move and feint as you get close.

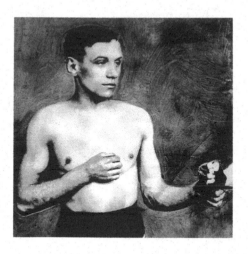

Commedia del Goalie

after Alan Salisbury

This is the goalkeeper's nightmare –
A late kick-off. Sharp end of the season.
The heavens stretch forever beyond the lights.
Hoots and whistles: it is the angels trumpeting derision
As they look down on his predicament.
He is rooted to the firmament.

Though he sprouts wings in emulation of their flight
He is tied to the ground, or suspended
In space so that the morning's back pages
Will immortalise his mistimed leap,
His cold, fumbling grasp: *Salisbury's Fatal Blunder.*

Everyone will remind him.
The breeze that rustles the slack side-netting
Conspires to form a skull.
In the cruel night air his knees wrinkle
Themselves into grins. He is the last man.

In the Commedia del Goalie, he is the clown,
The braying ass, the tragic Fool, the comic mime.
In the goal's mouth his boyhood dreams sour.
There is a penalty to be taken.
There will be no extra time.

Scrolling Down

11.04 5/11/2019

US sends missile system and ship to Gulf

Climate change may curb growth in flying

Venice: here's art on a staggering scale; some even good

Fight breaks out in Hong Kong parliament

Putin falls on ice after hockey match

Simon Armitage to be next Poet Laureate

Woman finds loaf full of bread crusts

Who was Gentleman Jack?

It's scary to see your mum handcuffed and taken away

Little surprises salvaged from museum ashes

Why the hairdressing salon got rid of mirrors

What can't you name your baby?

Make life-changing drug affordable – MPs.

Fun banned in playground as school breaks cut

How do you learn to drive on Mars?

The Four Minute Warning

They were always ahead of the clock —
Brasher first, Bannister second, Chataway third —
All the rest left behind and forgotten,
Bit-part actors, spear carriers behind three princes.

Four times round the oval track at Iffley Road,
The two pace men switching as planned, pavilion and stands
Packed with students in mackintoshes smoking, cadets,
And a smattering of girls taken out for an early May blow.

As he crossed the line and fell into the arms of his coach
Bannister could hear only the sound
Of a distant sea-shore of applause and cheers.
Now, at least, when the Bomb fell

And the mushroom blossomed over our land,
A man in those four minutes could run a mile.

Oxford 6th May, 1954: 3 mins. 59.4 secs, the world record.

Cinderella

So the young Ashton boy we met in Ecuador before the war
Is now quite the thing in London and the theatre.
His *Cinderella* was most affecting.
I swear I was close to tears at the poor girl's predicament
And then elated by her transformation as the belle of the ball,
As if one did not know the whole story.

We also saw his *Façade* at the Wells Theatre with Margot Fonteyn
And Robert Helpmann – most entertaining in an entirely lighthearted way.
And mercifully short.
The modern dances done with great wit and humour.
Frederick's talked of as a genius.
What on earth goes on inside the heads of the young?
That shy boy of eight was a dark horse – though always
This way inclined, I thought.

We had a brief word after the performance.
Frederick is one of four boys in the Ashton family,
The others, the practical ones, run the business
Now poor George has gone – in the most distressing circumstances.
Many a man is driven mad by the natives and the heat.
Frederick and the others must have been so badly shaken by that loss.
And Georgina left to cope in that large estate,
With servants and workers such a responsibility.

Next Saturday we sail back on the long voyage to Peru.
Those oilfields will not pump themselves, as Bill always says.

At the end of our visit that time to Guayaquil,
George Ashton offered us two slaves – a boy of seven
Already trained and his little sister of three.
A pretty thing with large, dark eyes.
They were to cost forty sucres for the boy and twenty for the girl.
No more than a handful of guineas then.
Those who buy them have to both feed and educate them.

I confess to being more than a little surprised by the offer.
In any case, we did not take them, we were well staffed in Lima.
But the poor things might have been better off with us, I suppose.
Another world, another time.
Whatever happens to such as those?

In the Duomo, Siracusa

For Helen Dunmore 28/6/17

A mother will always lift a child
as you knew at the last, Helen.
We are not in cloudy Bristol to say our goodbyes

but under the throbbing sun of Sicily
taking shelter, as we'd planned, in the duomo
this morning at the time of your funeral in your cathedral.

Here Saint Lucia in silver and gold is paraded
twice yearly through Ortygia borne by worthies.
Knowing, grounded Catholic,

you would have smiled: in the dish she holds
those are eyes that were her eyes;
from her stigmata-ed neck protrudes

an impossible dagger. Resolute, bejeweled virgin
who would give up neither her body or her faith:
it is a standard narrative of martyrdom.

You would have admired the flexed muscles of the gravediggers
Carravagio wrought with such life
as the fragile young priest performs his rites over prone Lucia.

The breath of my people drawn in pain.
This was your final lesson.
Oh, much closer to you would be Our Lady of the Snow,

this pure white marble Mother and Child, in the Norman apse,
a colder, clearer vision you'd welcome at the last.
Madonna della neve: we are people of the North.

It is cool here, and for a moment, quite still;
away from the baking Piazza, the crowds,
we'll hold our thoughts and memories as you go

out of the body in death, that motherly caress,
the waiting over, knowing your depth
and it's taking you in.

Last walk at Lydstep

The village is locked-down
but only I can tell tonight, I'm the only
witness to the dark, still lane and the closed pub.
From across the fields I can hear the sea.

Lights glow in a few homes, but the swings
and tennis nets at Celtic Haven Holidays
are slack and unused, the freshly painted
houses and stable blocks will be empty this season.

The place had been a turkey farm which supplied the *QE2*
and my mother; each Christmas for two decades
she'd drive up to us with a bird on the back seat.
Mum died years back and the house sale's going through.

Eleven years ago to the week, Withybush Hospital,
in her ninety-first year. As it should be.
Her heart gave out as ours dare not do
with the hospitals full to breaking now.

So many stars tonight in a perfect, black sky
that brings light from dead worlds and past times.
And stars at my feet – the first flush of wild garlic
with its fresh stink of sweet/sour breath

announcing the cruellest month.
My aunt Annie, the Pembrokeshire charmer,
would have been out foraging and wrenching them up
to gather the bulbs for potions and cures.

Warts, agues and women's troubles: for pennies
she ministered to family and neighbours.
A farm girl before the First War, the plague of 'Nineteen,
then an ex-soldier's wife, a smallholding near Kilgetty.

There's the Plough, Orion's Belt, the North Star,
and countless others I don't recognise.
No winking lights from the transatlantic planes,
now we are shrinking into ourselves, cancelled flights,

the world curling back into itself
for safety, and in fear.
This is the reckoning point, the date,
all manner of events and lives will be defined by this year.

Though the fields at the back of us are newly ploughed,
a flurry of gulls and crows jabbing at the fresh worms;
this afternoon there were hens let loose and scattered
across the empty road. One perched on our wall.

This county's a long way from anywhere,
and closed to visitors now: the police run checks.
Our Headland's been an Iron Age promontory fort,
a narrow strip to defend with the sea at your back.

In the war, mum's friend Reg had held a rope
over the edge near Whitesheet Rock above the crashing sea
for school mates to raid the crevice nests for gulls' eggs.
'Big and rich, but tasting of fish. Still, we was so hungry.'

Visiting the Big Man

At school I'd see him power over the line
with half the opposition pack scattered
and the others still clinging to him,
the rest of us trailing behind:
half a century ago.

In his yard at the house on Wooden Hill
just the two of us that day,
talking of school days and where we'd been,
he smoking one, though by this time it wasn't allowed.

And then the other side of the turfed wall
an almighty squawking and commotion –
'That damned fox again,' he said.
But all we saw in the coop was a scattering of feathers,
some blood and the hens, heads back down,
about their business.

We looked across the fields
for what had gone
and what we'd never see again.

That would have been the last time
I saw him, or maybe the time
before the last time.

Further instructions

It will surely be the end of a day –
early May on the cusp of spring and summer.
An evening refreshed by sun and wind
after rain has cleared the view across to Gower
and Pendine sands to the east,
Tenby clustered around the spike of St Mary's.

Best to take a line directly from the fifth tee
through that red-blinking buoy
to the white dome of the Caldey lighthouse.
You'll cross to the mid-point from buoy to shore
and have him idle the engine,
keeping the bow aimed at St Margaret's Island
to take the tide's run.
Then swing gently so that from the leeward
you can let spill what remains of me.

Watch the cormorant plotting parallel lines low
a foot or so it seems above the sea,
stitching his invisible net over
the clustered silver and blue of mackerel
frantic and fierce, above the pollock and bass;

This is the sea that David Jones,
at peace with the monks,
cut into wood as a bay of calm
beyond the grazing cows.

Around the fifth and thirteenth tees
the small fists of purple orchid
will have pushed through the heather
and the sharp and buttery gorse.
Someone waiting to play might drift
and turn to take in the view:
see the smudge of a boat out fishing
and that will quicken the heart.

A narrative

the beginning and the end of it
the enemy and friend of it

the good and the bad of it
the joy and the sad of it

the wanting to stay
the going away

the dreams forsaken
the roads not taken

the pull and the push of it
the blur and the rush of it

the people we met on the way
the places we could not stay

the length and the breadth of it
the reach and the depth of it

the warmth and the cold of it
our loosening hold on it

the moments that leaked away
the words we couldn't quite say

the mothers and fathers of all
the houses we lived in that fall

the soil that we dug, the flowers we grew
the vases we filled, the pictures we drew

the seeds that were blown
the weeds we hacked down

our desperate trust in it
the gleam then the rust of it

the sense of illusion
the need for conclusion

the steam and the huff involved
the mess and the stuff that evolved

the footnotes and references found
the Contents and Index bound

the friends and the close ones we choose
the close ones and friends that we lose

the patterns and shapes to see
the final lack of clarity

the strengthening tug of belief
the incoming tide of grief

the need to confess
the whole damn mess

Visitors

These are not swallows
but bats cutting through
the edges of the night,

grey smudges, then sharp angles
of flying geometry – call them pipistrelles –
the first at our new house.

They are swallowing the air
and this evening's midges
by the mouthful.

They are cleaning the sky
for us, aerial hawking,
measuring the garden, beating the bounds,

This is their ground, their air.
It must be the closeness of the woods,
Mount Ida, Llanblethian Hill.

Their squeaks and calls
are not within our hearing.
We cannot know what they say or think.

Not blind, but seeing enough
to live by.
They show us how it's done.

October Moon

Past midnight you sit up and say, "The moon."
We'd forgotten that tonight it's promised to be
As bright and full as ever this year –
Ninety-eight point seven.

Hand in hand we walk across the landing to your study –
Nothing. Too cloudy, barely a star.
And then try the front bedroom which shows a lighter sky
Than we would expect. The road is clear
And there's an aura, our neighbours' roofs magical.

Back in our bedroom we open the curtains my side of the bed,
Then, both kneeling as at prayer,
Angle up our gaze to take in the gable end next door,
And there's the full moon shining and clear –
A near perfect disc, a harvest moon, no, a hunter's –

Terms that used to have meaning in our world,
And are carried still in this silver coin,
This eye, a jewel, a glittering porcelain plate.
Below our hill, over the town,
We know the channel will be a shining lake.

After fifty years together yes, of course, hand in hand,
We go back to our bed and nothing's said
Or needed to be said, it seems.
We journey on through night and dreams.

Acknowledgements

"Leaving the Hills" concerns Aldous Huxley's time in California. In the Bel Air fire of 1961, he and his wife had to flee for their lives. There are many photos online of this event, including scenes of Richard Nixon and Kim Novak with water hoses on their respective roofs. This poem was published in Acumen.

"Of Barnacles, Geese and other Wonders" – Gerald of Wales reported back to Henry II. Such prejudiced stereotypes of Irish customs and beliefs helped to justify the English invasion as a civilizing mission, which suited royal and papal strategies.

"Caroline Gerbola on Conchita" is from Peter Lavery's exhibition of circus photographs. It was taken in Tralee, Ireland, in 1986 with the Fossett Brothers Circus.

"At the G6 Face" is a painting by Jack Crabtree in the University of South Wales collection.

"Aberfan Voices" was written in 2016 for the fiftieth anniversary of the disaster as a collaborative bi-lingual project with Grahame Davies. Our poems were in response to the 1996 photographs by Chuck Rapoport. Some of mine were featured in Dai Smith's Radio Wales programme. Also published by Goddard College's Clockhouse magazine in Vermont.

"Where I was" was read as part of the Welsh Senedd's day of remembrance.

"Dannie's Rock" – two of the important influences on me are referenced; in addition to Dannie Abse, there is a Vernon Watkins-inspired closing image; see his poem "The Feather".

"Flying the Lanner" appeared as The Friday Poem on the website thefridaypoem.com in June, 2021.

"Claude and Chouchou at Le Moulleau, 1916" was included in Poems from Pandemia, Southword/ Munster Poetry Festival book, 2020. Both Claude Debussy and his daughter died shortly afterwards.

"Madame des Lapins" is thanks to Jane and Alan Salisbury, who are bi-located in Wales and France.

"The Trials of Anne James" – sourced from a document used by the University of Melbourne Law Faculty. One of the witnesses in the court at Haverfordwest was my Pembrokeshire ancestor, James Barrah.

"The Rising of the Rivers" was included in the book and website of Fred Jones's A Journal of the Sacred, Spiritual and the Sublime in Nature, Illinois 2022. Also published online by The Blue Nib.

"David Nash – Crack and Warp Column" was published in the RA Magazine, November, 2019.

"Nature to Nature" appeared in the Friends of the National Museum of Wales Newsletter, Jan, 2020.

"Poems for the painter Hanlyn Davies in New England" was a contribution to The Vein of Lice, a consideration of the artist's work published in the USA by Silver Street Media, 2018.

"Leather Chair with a Portrait of Marion" was written for the Interior Monologues exhibition at the University of South Wales in February 2019. "A Jazz Suite" was published by The High Window magazine in 2023.

"The Song Prize" was at the Cardiff Singer of the World Competition, in St David's Hall, in 2019, where I'd heard Brubeck play in 2003.

"Commedia del Goalie" is in response to a painting by Alan Salisbury and was written for his retrospective exhibition at the University of South Wales.

"The Four Minute Warning" – three students, who all went on to significant professional careers, achieved this remarkable feat. Sir Roger Bannister, who became a leading neurologist, sharpened his spikes at St. Mary's Hospital before catching the train from London to Oxford. There was no four-minute warning sounded. No nuclear bomb was dropped. The Iffley Road athletics stadium is now named after him.

"Naming Jimmy Wilde" was published in The Lonely Crowd magazine in 2024.

"Cinderella" concerns the family background of Sir Frederick Ashton (1904-1988), Britain's most notable dancer and choreographer.

"Last Walk at Lydstep" was a Seren Press Poem of the Week in 2020 and was recorded for the Poetry Archive on YouTube that year. It was included in the anthology Poems for the Year 2020 edited by Merryn Williams, Shoestring Press, 2021.

"Visiting the Big Man" concerns a school friend from Tenby, Mervyn James John, whose passing was marked by two poems in From the Fortunate Isles – "St. Elidyr's, Amroth" and "Amroth in October".

"Further Instructions" appeared in my Real South Pembrokeshire, Seren, 2011.

"Belgian Hares" and "That July in Charleston" were read by the poet on the Poetry Worth Hearing podcast, number 20. https://podcasters.spotify.com/pod/show/kathleen-mcphilemy.

Some poems were first published in: Poetry Wales, Planet, Stand, The Lonely Crowd, The North, Poetry Ireland Review. Online: The Blue Nib, Verbal Art, ASP Magazine. and Quill and Parchment.

About the Author

Tony Curtis was born in Carmarthen in 1946 and grew up there and in Pembrokeshire, where his grandmother's family had lived for hundreds of years.

He read English at Swansea University, did an MFA in Goddard College, Vermont and spent forty years in education, from 1969 to 2009, as a school teacher then a college lecturer and as Wales's first Professor of Poetry at the University of Glamorgan, where he developed and directed the M. Phil in Writing.

He has written and edited over forty books, most recently his first novel *Darkness in the City of Light* and an anthology of poems for the Ty Hafan children's charity – *Where the Birds Sing our Names*.

He was given a Gregory Award in 1972; he won the National Poetry Competition in 1983. In 1993, he won the Dylan Thomas Award for Spoken Poetry, judged by Dannie Abse and Dylan's daughter Aeronwy. He received a Cholmondeley Award in 1998. He was awarded a D.Litt. in 2004. He is a Fellow of the Royal Society of Literature.

A full bibliography and biography may be found at tonycurtispoet.com